Idaho

BY MARGARET LAWLER

CONTENT CONSULTANT
Sarah Phillips, MA
Curator of Collections and Exhibitions
Idaho State Historical Society

Core Library

An Imprint of Abdo Publishing
abdobooks.com

abdobooks.com

Printed in the United States of America, North Mankato, Minnesota.
052022
092022

THIS BOOK CONTAINS
RECYCLED MATERIALS

Cover Photo: Shutterstock Images
Interior Photos: Jim Cottingham/Shutterstock Images, 4, 19 (garnets); Steven Andrews, 4–5; Red
Line Editorial, 6 (Idaho), 6 (USA); Kris Wiktor/Shutterstock Images, 10–11, 43; Barry Kough/Lewiston
Tribune/AP Images, 12; Shutterstock Images, 16–17, 19 (flag), 19 (flower), 19 (horse), 40; Tom
Reichner/Shutterstock Images, 19 (bird); C. S. Nafzger/Shutterstock Images, 22–23, 26, 45; Kirk
Fisher/Shutterstock Images, 30–31; Denton Rumsey/Shutterstock Images, 33; Cameron Spencer/
Getty Images Sport/Getty Images, 36–37

Editor: Marie Pearson
Series Designer: Joshua Olson

Library of Congress Control Number: 2021951396

Publisher's Cataloging-in-Publication Data

Names: Lawler, Margaret, author.
Title: Idaho / by Margaret Lawler
Description: Minneapolis, Minnesota : Abdo Publishing, 2023 | Series: Core library of US states |
    Includes online resources and index.
Identifiers: ISBN 9781532197536 (lib. bdg.) | ISBN 9781098270292 (ebook)
Subjects: LCSH: U.S. states--Juvenile literature. | Western States (U.S.)--Juvenile literature. | Idaho--
    History--Juvenile literature. | Physical geography--United States--Juvenile literature.
Classification: DDC 979.6--dc23

Population demographics broken down by race and ethnicity come from the 2019 census estimate.
Population totals come from the 2020 census.

CONTENTS

THE GEM STATE

P eople are looking for star garnets near a streambed in Idaho. These purplish-red stones are Idaho's state gem. They are rare. Idaho is one of only two places in the world where people can find star garnets. Idaho is nicknamed the Gem State. Its lands hold more than 70 different types of gemstones.

People scoop some gravel into buckets. When their buckets are full, they carefully dump the contents into pans. The pans have

Some people enjoy looking for star garnets at Emerald Creek Garnet Area.

MAP OF
IDAHO

Idaho is known for its natural spaces. How does this map help you understand Idaho's geography?

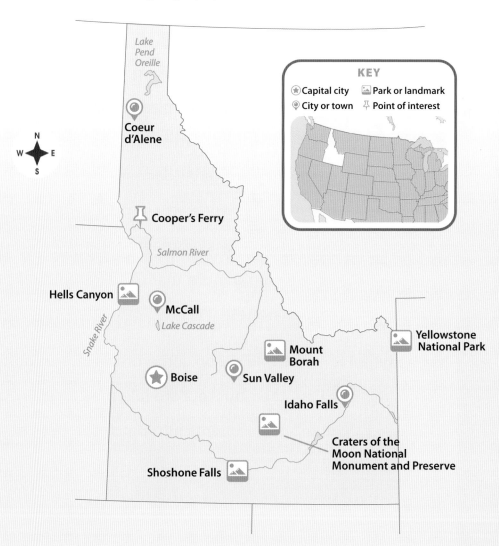

KEY

⊛ Capital city   🖼 Park or landmark
⦿ City or town   ⊼ Point of interest

Lake Pend Oreille

Coeur d'Alene

Cooper's Ferry

Salmon River

Hells Canyon

McCall

Lake Cascade

Snake River

Mount Borah

Yellowstone National Park

Boise

Sun Valley

Idaho Falls

Craters of the Moon National Monument and Preserve

Shoshone Falls

holes in the bottom. Dirt and small rocks trickle through the holes. Once the people are done sifting out the dirt, all that remains are the larger rocks. After rinsing the rocks with water, they discover a few gleaming star garnets.

EXPLORING IDAHO

Idaho is part of the region called the West. Like other states in this region, Idaho has mountains. It also has beautiful forests. Idaho's mountains are part of the Rocky Mountain Range. Winter snows bring

CRATERS OF THE MOON

Volcanoes have shaped part of Idaho's landscape. Craters of the Moon National Monument and Preserve showcases rocky fields and caves. Volcano eruptions starting 15,000 years ago created these structures. Kipukas can be found among the cooled volcanic rocks. Kipukas are patches of higher ground that were protected from the lava flows. Plants such as sagebrush grow on the kipukas. Craters of the Moon is located in south-central Idaho. It covers more than 1,100 square miles (2,800 sq km). This is approximately the same size as Rhode Island.

skiers and snowboarders to the slopes. People enjoy camping in Idaho's evergreen forests. Deserts make up large parts of southern Idaho.

Six states border Idaho. Washington and Oregon lie west of Idaho. Nevada and Utah are along the state's southern border. Wyoming and Montana are to the east. Canada borders Idaho to the north.

Idaho's big cities feature plenty of outdoor getaways. Boise is the largest city in the state. It is also the state's capital. Many big companies have offices there. People enjoy bike rides along the shores of the Boise River. They can also rock climb at the Black Cliffs nearby. Idaho Falls is located on the eastern side of the state. It is a short drive from Yellowstone National Park and Grand Teton National Park in Wyoming. Coeur d'Alene is a popular tourist destination in the state. The city sits next to Lake Coeur d'Alene, and there are more than 55 other nearby lakes. These lakes were created by glaciers.

Some towns provide access to outdoor fun. Sun Valley and McCall are popular among skiers and snowboarders. These towns also offer hiking, fishing, and other outdoor activities.

In addition to having many beautiful natural sites, Idaho is one of the fastest-growing states in the country. Idaho's population began growing quickly in the 2010s. People move to the state for the natural beauty and other opportunities Idaho has to offer.

PERSPECTIVES

POPULATION GROWTH

In 2018 nearly 80,000 people moved to Idaho. Most newcomers came from nearby states, including California, Washington, and Utah. Idaho's low cost of living and access to outdoor activities make it an attractive place to live. Todd Shallat was a professor at Boise State University. He moved to Boise more than 30 years ago. He described why he and many others have moved to the city. "It's the myth of the empty," Shallat said. "Most of us came from places that had crowds. We envisioned [Boise] as a frontier."

HISTORY
OF IDAHO

People have lived in Idaho for more than 16,000 years. Historians believe these early peoples sailed inland on rivers that connected to the Pacific Ocean. They then settled near what is now called the Salmon River at a site now known as Cooper's Ferry. The people living in this location may have been some of the first people to live in North America.

Over time, people spread across the land and created different cultures. The Nimiipuu (Nez Perce) people lived at Cooper's Ferry,

Idaho's rivers, including the Salmon River, were important sources of food and transportation for the first people in the region.

Nimiipuu (Nez Perce) people continue to live in Idaho. Some Nimiipuu students, including Glory Sobotta, *right*, have written books that highlight Nimiipuu culture.

which they called Nipéhe. They lived in parts of Idaho

as well as other regions in the Pacific Northwest. The

Nimiipuu traded with nations such as the Schitsu'umsh

(Coeur D'Alene). The Schitsu'umsh lived in northern

Idaho, where they built villages beside rivers. Canoeing along these rivers allowed them to trade with other nations in the Pacific Northwest.

The Shoshone lived in southern Idaho. The Bannock later came to this region and began hunting bison with the Shoshone. The Bannock are related to the Northern Paiutes of present-day Nevada and Utah. The Nimiipuu, Schitsu'umsh, Shoshone-Bannock, Shoshone-Paiute, and Kootenai continue to live in Idaho. They belong to the American Indian nations in Idaho that the US government recognizes today.

EUROPEAN ARRIVAL

Spanish explorers were the first Europeans to arrive in or near Idaho. They came in the late 1500s and began trading with the American Indian peoples. The Spanish traded horses. The horses made it easier for American Indian peoples, including the Shoshone and the Bannock, to hunt bison.

American explorers Meriwether Lewis and William Clark entered the Idaho region in 1805. At the time this region did not officially belong to the United States. They mapped the rivers and mountains in the region. They noticed the land had many beavers. Beaver furs could be used to make hats. People began arriving in Idaho to make money from the fur trade.

French fur trappers arrived soon afterward. Many of them came from Canada. They traded with the Schitsu'umsh, whom they called the Coeur d'Alene. This translates to "Heart of the Awl." An awl is a sharp

HISTORIC TRAIL

In 1803 the United States purchased a large area of land from the French. Lewis and Clark led an expedition through the new land. Though the purchase did not include Idaho, the explorers entered the region in 1805. They met Shoshone people who led them along a difficult trail that crossed the Bitterroot Mountains. People today can visit this historic trail. It extends through 11 states, including Idaho. It is called the Lewis and Clark National Historic Trail.

tool that can punch holes in wood and leather. The French gave the Schitsu'umsh this name because of the people's sharp trading skills.

The United States and Great Britain signed a treaty in 1818. They agreed to share the Pacific Northwest region. British subjects and American settlers shared the area until 1846. By this time most people in the region were American. The two countries signed the Treaty of Oregon. This gave the United States sole control of the land that would later become Idaho, Oregon, and Washington.

As a result of the fur industry and the arrival of new settlers, conflicts between settlers and American Indians increased. Tensions arose again after gold was discovered in California in 1849. Many people traveled through the area to get to California. Idaho then had its own gold rush in the 1860s. The Boise Basin Gold Rush brought thousands of people into the area. Conflicts broke out as white settlers edged into American

Silver City is an abandoned town that formed in the 1860s during the gold rush.

Indian homelands. The growing population of settlers led the US government to create the Idaho Territory in 1863.

The US government forced nations including the Nimiipuu to sign treaties and give up the land they

had lived on for generations. The US government
moved American Indians to reservations. Over time
the US government began reducing the size of some
reservations in order to allow more settlers to search
for gold. To protect their land, the Nimiipuu fought
the US Army in the Nez Perce War of 1877. But the

Nimiipuu were unsuccessful. The US government forced them out of Idaho for several years. The government allowed them to return to their homelands in the mid-1880s.

STATEHOOD

The Northern Pacific Railroad was completed in 1882. Railroads made it easy to transport goods such as crops from Idaho to other states. They also allowed people to get to Idaho more quickly. Then in 1884 there was another mining boom. Zinc, lead, silver, and phosphate became major mining products. With a booming population, Idaho became the forty-third state on July 3, 1890.

Idaho has three branches of government. The legislative branch has elected officials. These officials create, change, and vote on bills. The executive branch includes an elected governor. Governors can choose to sign bills into law. The third branch is the judicial branch. This branch includes the system of courts in Idaho.

IDAHO
QUICK FACTS

There are lots of things that make Idaho unique. Why do you think these facts and symbols are a point of pride for Idaho's residents?

Abbreviation: ID
Nickname: The Gem State
Motto: *Esto perpetua* (Be eternal)
Date of statehood: July 3, 1890
Capital: Boise
Population: 1,839,106
Area: 83,569 square miles (216,443 sq km)

STATE SYMBOLS

State bird
Mountain bluebird

State gem
Idaho star garnet

State flower
Syringa (mock orange)

State horse
Appaloosa

Idaho played an important role in World War II (1939–1945). The US government constructed the Farragut Naval Training Station. Soldiers began training there in 1942. At the time it was the second-largest US naval training station in the world. Military influence continued after the end of the war. The Idaho National Laboratory opened in 1949. It was a nuclear testing site. It was also one of the first sites to make electricity using nuclear energy. In the 1970s Idaho National Laboratory began researching other types of energy.

The region of Idaho has a long history. American Indian nations, European explorers, and US settlers have shaped the state into what it is today. Idaho's population continues to grow. The people living in the state today are molding Idaho's future.

EXPLORE ONLINE

Chapter Two discusses Cooper's Ferry. The article at the website below goes into more depth on this topic. Does the article answer any of the questions you had about Idaho's early history?

NEW ARTIFACTS SUGGEST FIRST PEOPLE ARRIVED IN NORTH AMERICA EARLIER THAN PREVIOUSLY THOUGHT

abdocorelibrary.com/idaho

GEOGRAPHY AND CLIMATE

Idaho is a large state with many landforms. The Rocky Mountains cover much of the state. Central Idaho has the highest peaks. The state has nine mountain peaks that are higher than 12,000 feet (3,700 m). This includes Mount Borah, which is Idaho's highest point in elevation. It stands 12,662 feet (3,859 m) above sea level.

Plateaus formed along the Idaho-Wyoming border. These are flat areas with high elevation. Idaho's plateaus are covered in grasses and sagebrush.

Idaho has beautiful mountains and valleys.

Southeastern Idaho is part of the Basin and Range Province. This region covers most of Nevada and also extends into Utah and California. The climate is dry and desertlike. The region is prone to earthquakes. Earth's crust is divided into large sections called plates. The places where plates meet are called fault lines. The plates move and rub against each other at the fault lines, causing earthquakes. The Basin and Range Province has several fault lines.

Southwestern Idaho has canyons. Hells Canyon is the deepest in North America. It is even deeper than the Grand Canyon.

More than 40 percent of the state is forested. Idaho has more than 21.5 million acres (8.7 million ha) of forest. The US government protects some of Idaho's forests. The largest of these is the Salmon-Challis National Forest in the central part of the state.

Idaho also has several major rivers. The Snake River flows through Idaho for 779 miles (1,254 km).

It is the longest river in the state. The river winds through lava fields and cascades into waterfalls, such as Shoshone Falls. This waterfall is taller than Niagara Falls.

Idaho's lakes also attract tourists. Lake Pend Oreille is the largest and deepest lake in the state. Glaciers formed the lake millions of years ago during the last ice age. Lake Cascade is another famous Idaho lake. It is located 75 miles (120 km) north of Boise. Lake Cascade is one of the largest lakes in Idaho.

PERSPECTIVES
EVEL KNIEVEL

The Snake River forms the Snake River Canyon. People enjoy hiking and extreme sports such as BASE jumping here. BASE jumping is when people parachute off a cliff or other tall structure. The Snake River Canyon also attracted famous daredevil and motorcycle stuntman Evel Knievel in 1974. He attempted to leap over the canyon in a steam-powered motorcycle that looked like a rocket. It would have been a 0.25-mile (0.4-km) jump. But his parachute opened too early, and Knievel fell into the canyon. He survived the attempt with only a broken nose.

Idaho has scenic slopes for snowboarding and skiing.

Visitors enjoy camping on beaches and windsurfing. Those who like fishing can catch trout and salmon at the lake.

CLIMATE

Idaho's geography affects its climate and weather. As elevation rises, temperatures tend to be cooler. Areas with high elevation also tend to get more rain and snow. Westerly winds from the Pacific Ocean keep northern and southwestern Idaho warmer. In contrast, southeastern Idaho tends to be cooler.

Tall mountains in Oregon and Washington block moisture that comes from the Pacific Ocean. Lower elevations do not get much rain. As a result, some areas of Idaho are considered desertlike. A few areas, such as the northern Rockies, get a lot of snowfall. Sun Valley is a resort town for skiing. In 2019 the town broke its record for February snowfall. It received more than 10 feet (3 m) of snow.

PLANTS AND ANIMALS

Idaho's many geographic regions are home to a wide range of plants and animals. The state tree, the western white pine, can be found in the northern part of the state. Some of Idaho's plants cannot be found anywhere else. An example is Sacajawea's bitterroot. It is named after Sacajawea, a Shoshone woman who helped lead Lewis and Clark through Idaho. This small flowering plant grows mainly in Boise National Forest but is also found in other Idaho forests. It grows at high elevations. Blooms come soon after the snow melts.

Idaho's state flower also has ties to the Lewis and Clark expedition. Lewis described the white flowers of the syringa, or mock orange, in his journal.

BUG CONTROL

Idaho has 14 species of bats. Bats are important animals. Many eat insects that carry harmful diseases or destroy crops. Some bats travel to and from the state by season. Others stay in Idaho all year long. The little brown bat is one species that stays all year. It eats moths, mosquitoes, and flies. In the winter, little brown bats hibernate in caves.

American Indians in the region used branches from the shrub to make bows and arrows.

Pygmy rabbits live in the sagebrush fields of the Middle Rockies. They are the smallest rabbits in North America. Pygmy rabbits rely on the sagebrush for food and shelter.

The mountain bluebird is Idaho's state bird. It can handle colder temperatures than other types of bluebirds. Idaho also has a state raptor, the peregrine falcon. This falcon is pictured on Idaho's state quarter. The large bird can dive through the air at 200 miles per hour (320 km/h) to catch prey. It is considered one of the fastest animals on Earth.

STRAIGHT TO THE
SOURCE

The Mount Borah earthquake in 1983 was one of the largest earthquakes recorded in Idaho. It caused more than $12.5 million in damage. Geologists Steven W. Moore and R. David Hovland described the earthquake in an article:

> *Suddenly, the peaceful mountain morning was shattered as powerful forces within the earth's crust were unleashed. Normal morning activities were interrupted as windowpanes vibrated and alarmed people ran out of their houses. . . .*
>
> *Ground shaking was most intense . . . between Challis and Mackay, but the earthquake was also felt over most of the northwestern United States and in parts of Canada.*

Source: Steven W. Moore and R. David Hovland. "The Borah Peak Earthquake." *Digital Atlas of Idaho*, n.d., digitalatlas.cose.isu.edu. Accessed 16 Apr. 2021.

CONSIDER YOUR AUDIENCE

Adapt this passage for a different audience, such as your younger friends. Write a blog post conveying this same information to the new audience. How does your post differ from the original text and why?

RESOURCES AND ECONOMY

Idaho is known for its rich natural resources. Historically, silver and gold brought many people to the state. Silver mining continues to be an important part of Idaho's economy. In addition, Idaho is a major producer of lead and phosphate. Phosphate is a mineral that is most commonly used in fertilizers, which help plants grow.

Agriculture is another one of Idaho's major industries. The state has more than 25,000 farms and ranches. The industry makes

Wallace has been a silver-mining town for more than 100 years.

31

ROCKHOUNDING

The Gem State is an attractive location for rockhounding. This is the activity of collecting rocks, gemstones, and fossils. Rock hounds don't need a permit to hunt for rocks on public land, but the US Bureau of Land Management does have rules for the activity. For example, rock hounds are not allowed to use explosives to unearth rocks. The rocks they collect cannot be sold commercially. Rock hounds also need to make sure that they search only on public lands. They could be jailed for removing rocks from privately owned lands.

up approximately 28 percent of the state's economy. The state is most famous for its potatoes. It is the leading producer of potatoes in the United States. Nearly one-third of the country's potato crops grow here. Idaho also produces large amounts of wheat, barley, sugar beets, and mint.

Livestock brings in the most money of any agricultural industry. Idaho's cattle and sheep graze on large areas of grassland. Many of the cows are raised for dairy and milk production. Idaho's cows produce more than

Potatoes grow in large farm fields in Idaho.

1.51 billion gallons (5.7 billion L) of milk every year. Idaho is also the third-largest producer of cheese in the United States.

TECHNOLOGY AND ENERGY

Idaho's economy has continued to develop over the years. Technology is one of Idaho's growing industries. Hewlett-Packard makes products such as software, computers, and printers. Its printing division is based in Idaho. In 2018 the Idaho Department of Labor projected that the number of tech jobs in the state would increase by 45 percent over the next ten years.

With an expanding economy, energy needs are also growing. Researchers at the Idaho National Laboratory study nuclear energy. The laboratory is one of the most important nuclear research centers in the United States.

Idaho has sources of renewable energy too. Renewable energy comes from sources other than coal, oil, or gas. Hydroelectricity is the largest source of renewable energy in the state. It comes from running water.

For example, dams on the Snake River turn the water's movement into electricity.

Southern Idaho has sources of geothermal energy. This type of energy comes from magma deep underground. The magma heats underground water, which releases steam that can be captured and used as an energy source. Volcanoes formed Idaho's landscape long ago. Because of this, the state has a lot of geothermal energy sources. People can use geothermal energy to heat homes and businesses.

FURTHER EVIDENCE

Chapter Four discusses Idaho's economy. What was one of the main points of this chapter? What evidence is included to support this point? Read the article at the website below. Does the information on the website support the main point of the chapter? Does it present new evidence?

CROPS GROWN IN IDAHO
abdocorelibrary.com/idaho

PEOPLE AND PLACES

daho is home to many famous people. Its mountain landscape has helped develop winter athletes such as Jessika Jenson. She was born in Idaho Falls and competed in snowboarding at the 2014 and 2018 Winter Olympics. Football player Taysom Hill was also born and raised in Idaho.

DEMOGRAPHICS

More than 80 percent of Idaho's population is white people who are not Hispanic or Latino. Historically, French fur trappers settled in the area. French influence is still seen in the

Jessika Jenson placed fifth in the slopestyle event in the 2018 Winter Olympics.

GOLDEN CYCLIST

Kristin Armstrong has won more cycling races than any other American woman. Armstrong went to college in Idaho. She stayed after she graduated. She is the only female US athlete to win the same event at three Olympic Games in a row. Armstrong won gold for the time trial event in 2008, 2012, and 2016. The 2016 win marked another milestone. She became the oldest female cyclist to win an Olympic medal.

names of many Idaho cities and towns. For example, Boise comes from the French words *le bois*, which mean "the woods." Boise today is nicknamed the City of Trees.

Nearly 13 percent of Idaho's population is Hispanic or Latino. Between 2010 and 2019, the Hispanic population grew by 30.5 percent. This was a higher rate than that of Idaho's total population, which experienced a 14 percent growth.

The American Indian population makes up less than 2 percent of the state. There are five federally recognized tribes in Idaho. Some American Indians live on reservations with people of the same nation. Others live in cities or rural areas. Some tribal nations hold cultural celebrations called powwows. They may invite others to come and learn more about their cultures. The Shoshone-Bannock tribe has held an annual powwow since 1964. The people celebrate their culture through food, dancing, and other events.

ACTIVITIES

Idahoans know the importance of getting outside. Idaho has more than 20 state parks.

PERSPECTIVES
YOUNG HISPANIC VOTERS

Hispanic people make up approximately 7 percent of Idaho's voters. As the Hispanic population has grown in Idaho, politicians are becoming more aware of representing this demographic. Hispanic youth know that voting is one way of making their voices heard. Merci Vargas is Idaho's state president of the organization Future Hispanic Leaders of America. She said, "I realized my vote really matters, and it can change anything."

Lava flows and cinder cones give an otherworldly look to
Craters of the Moon National Monument and Preserve.

Yellowstone National Park is partially in the state.
Visitors to Craters of the Moon National Monument and
Preserve get an up-close look at Idaho's volcanic past.

Hiking and canoeing are popular in the
summertime. Mountains offer exciting snowboarding,
skiing, and snowshoeing opportunities. People also
enjoy soaking in Idaho's hot springs. From big cities
to wide-open spaces, Idaho has an adventure waiting
for everyone.

STRAIGHT TO THE
SOURCE

Today some American Indians live on reservations. They have histories with the land far longer than the United States has been a country. On the Coeur d'Alene Tribe's website, the Schitsu'umsh (Coeur d'Alene) people describe their connection with the land:

> *The old ones walked here. Those yet unborn will walk here, too. From a tribal perspective, the Coeur d'Alene presence here on the reservation and within the ancient homeland has lasted from the beginning of time. Every tribal member knows and feels the link to generations past. The culture and traditions have developed and been passed on for thousands of years—in the same place. In modern Indians, you see the faces of their ancestors.*

Source: "Environment." *Coeur d'Alene Tribe*, n.d., cdatribe-nsn.gov. Accessed 7 May 2021.

WHAT'S THE BIG IDEA?

Take a close look at this passage. What is the main connection being made between the land and the Schitsu'umsh who live there? What can you tell about their relationship with the land? Does the excerpt help you understand more about Schitsu'umsh history and culture?

IMPORTANT DATES

16,000 years ago
Early peoples settle in Idaho near the present-day Salmon River.

1500s CE
Spanish explorers arrive in the Idaho region.

1805
The first American explorers, including Meriwether Lewis and William Clark, enter the Idaho region.

1863
The US government creates the Idaho Territory.

1890
Idaho becomes the forty-third US state on July 3.

1949
The Idaho National Laboratory opens. It is an important site for nuclear research.

1974
Evel Knievel attempts to leap over the Snake River Canyon on a rocket-like motorcycle.

2010s
Idaho becomes one of the fastest-growing states in terms of population.

Tell the Tale

Chapter One of this book describes people hunting for gemstones. Imagine you are going rockhounding in Idaho. Write 200 words about the steps you take to find gemstones and the types of gemstones you discover.

Surprise Me

Chapter Two discusses the history of Idaho. After reading this book, what two or three facts about Idaho's history did you find most surprising? Write a few sentences about each fact. Why did you find each fact surprising?

Take a Stand

Evel Knievel attempted his daredevil stunt over the Snake River Canyon in 1974. Some people think these stunts are exciting forms of entertainment. Other people think the stunts are too dangerous and could cause severe injuries. Imagine you had the chance to see Evel Knievel perform. Would you go to watch his daring jump? Why or why not?

You Are There

This book discusses a few of the animals and plants that
live in Idaho. Imagine you are taking a hike through one of
Idaho's forests. Write a letter home telling your friends what
you have seen. What do you notice about the wildlife? Be
sure to add plenty of detail to your notes.

GLOSSARY

boom
a sudden, large increase in growth

culture
the way a group of people lives; its customs, beliefs, and laws

demographic
a division of a human population into categories, such as race

hibernate
to rest or sleep through the winter

mineral
a nonliving substance found naturally on Earth

nuclear
relating to the type of energy produced by splitting atoms; commonly associated with atomic bombs

reservation
an area of land set aside for American Indian people

species
a group of animals or plants that are similar and can reproduce

territory
an area of land that is not a state but is still controlled by a country

treaty
an official agreement between governments

ONLINE RESOURCES

To learn more about Idaho, visit our free resource websites below.

Visit **abdocorelibrary.com** or scan this QR code for free Common Core resources for teachers and students, including vetted activities, multimedia, and booklinks, for deeper subject comprehension.

Visit **abdobooklinks.com** or scan this QR code for free additional online weblinks for further learning. These links are routinely monitored and updated to provide the most current information available.

LEARN MORE

Wang, Yinan. *The 50 State Gems and Minerals: A Guidebook for Aspiring Geologists.* Schiffer, 2020.

Yasuda, Anita. *Exploring the West.* Abdo, 2018.

INDEX

About the Author

Margaret Lawler lives in Minnesota, where she edits and writes children's books. In her free time, she enjoys baking and playing board games.